An Average Day

Daily Routine, Road Safety and Visual Cards

V. Jean $ A. Jean

**Grosvenor House
Publishing Limited**

This book is published by
Grosvenor House Publishing Ltd
Link House
140 The Broadway, Tolworth, Surrey, KT6 7HT.
www.grosvenorhousepublishing.co.uk

This book is a work of fiction. Any resemblance to
people or events, past or present, is purely coincidental.

A CIP record for this book
is available from the British Library

ISBN 978-1-80381-388-2
eBook ISBN 978-1-80381-389-9

Dedicated to my magnificent family,
Akos, Kende and Akos.

Once upon a time, there was a beautiful, clever, creative and very kind little boy called Oliver. Oliver does not like rules; he has difficulty keeping up with everyday routines, which do not require any creative thought.
Therefore, Mummy has worked out a daily routine focusing on choices Oliver can make.
By using visual cards, Mummy is easing the transition from one activity to another. This is their average day.

"Good morning, Oliver," says Mummy, lovingly.
"Did you sleep well?"
"Yes I did," replies Oliver, still a bit sleepy.
"Let's go to the living room," says Mummy,
"you can have some screen time,
while I prepare your breakfast."

While Mummy prepares breakfast, Daddy sits
next to Oliver and they watch a cartoon together.
Soon, Daddy hugs and tells Oliver that he will
now go to work, but Oliver wants to stay home and
play with Mummy and Daddy.

"I am sorry, Oliver, but
Mummy and Daddy have to work
and you have to go to nursery,"
explains Daddy, then assures him
they will play together in the afternoon.

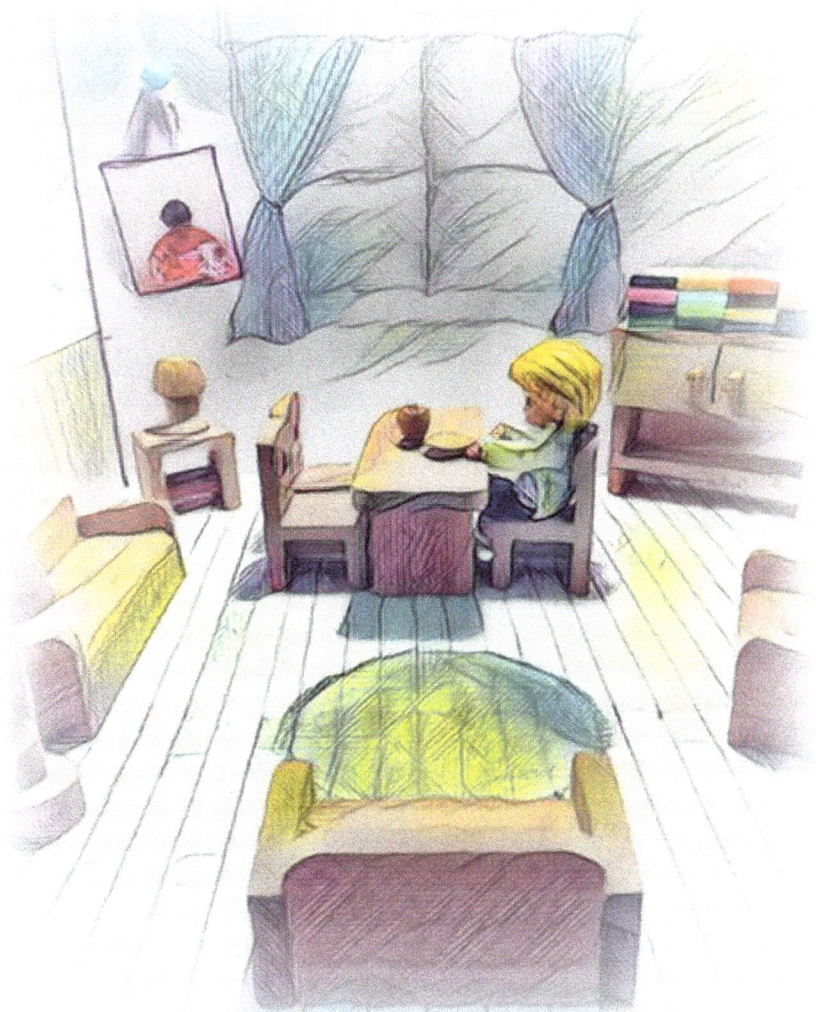

Mummy brings Oliver his breakfast
with a glass of vitamin smoothie.
"Enjoy your meal and have your smoothie,
sweetheart," says Mummy lovingly.

"I am filling your water bottle as well.
It is very important to drink plenty of water
during the day and eat healthy food.
This is how you grow big and strong,
like superheroes," says Mummy, winking at him.

"Now it is time to brush your teeth.
This needs to be done every morning
and every evening to avoid bad
and painful teeth," explains Mummy.
Oliver usually does not feel like brushing his teeth,
so Mummy gives him a choice of which toothbrush
he wants to use, the red or the blue one.
Oliver decides to use the red one.

After Oliver has brushed his teeth,
he independently uses the toilet and
washes his hands afterwards.
Mummy praises him and explains how
important it is to wash our hands to
avoid bad germs that can make us sick.

Mummy warns Oliver that he has to get dressed in five minutes. Mummy counts down to let Oliver know how many minutes are left: 4-3-2-1-0. Then Mummy puts two sets of clothes onto the sofa. Oliver chooses his t-shirt and trousers to wear for the day. Once dressed, they are ready to leave home.

On the way to the nursery, Mummy warns Oliver about road safety. "Look, we as pedestrians must go only on the pavement, while cars and buses must go on the road.

LOOK RIGHT

You must be very cautious when
you want to cross the road.
Always look right and left, and make sure
there is no vehicle approaching before
you step onto the road.

If there is a traffic light, always wait for
the green man traffic light signal.
Don't forget: red stop, green go!
Now it is your turn to show Mummy
how we can get safely to the nursery."

Oliver listens to Mummy and is very excited
about taking the lead and proving to Mummy
that he understands road safety.
Oliver takes Mummy's hand and says,
"Come on, Mummy, now we walk on the pavement."

When they reach a pedestrian crossing, Oliver says,
"Stop, Mummy! I press the button to show we want to
go across and wait for the green figure."
The cars stop and the light turns to green.
"Now we can cross safely, Mummy."

When they arrive at the nursery, Mummy feels really
proud of Oliver, so she praises him.
"You did a very great job!"
Mummy gives Oliver a big hug and many kisses.
Oliver feels very happy.

Oliver and Mummy step into the nursery and
welcome everyone they meet with a "Good morning!"
"Good morning, Oliver. How are you today?" replies
Oliver's teacher, smiling. And she then praises
him for being polite.

Mummy turns to Oliver and cuddles him.
"I love you," says Mummy and kisses him.
"Have a nice day, I will pick you up in the afternoon.
Don't forget, if you need to go to the toilet,
and need assistance, just tell one of your teachers."

Oliver really enjoys nursery.
He learns about letters and numbers.
They draw and paint amazing pictures.
Oliver always listens to the teachers
and follows their instructions.

At lunchtime, Oliver chooses healthy vegetables
and fruits, and eats all of them,
whilst drinking plenty of water.
"Well done, Oliver!" says the teacher
every time Oliver finishes his lunch.

During free play, there is a lot of fun
to be discovered, like playing in the sandpit,
climbing on a wooden house,
learning about sea life, or building train
tracks. Oliver loves them all.

In the afternoon, Mummy comes
to pick Oliver up from nursery.
"How was your day?" asks Mummy.
Oliver tells Mummy what happened
to him during the day.
Mummy listens to him with full attention.

Mummy asks Oliver if he wants to go for a walk,
or go to the playground before they go home.
Oliver chooses both. On the way, Oliver collects
many treasures, such as leaves and stones.

Mummy explains to Oliver how important and
beneficial it is to go and connect with nature
whenever it is possible. She tells him about trees,
and their important role of cleaning the air by
absorbing odours and polluting gases, and how
they release oxygen into the air.

After discussing the importance of trees,
Oliver and Mummy watch the ants work in
a very organised way, then talk about the important
role of bees. Mummy explains that bees collect pollen
and nectar as food for themselves,
and as they do, they pollinate plants.

"By pollinating plants, we can have most of our healthy food and vegetables. However, there are other insects, birds, and bats too, who help in this pollinating process. People need to learn to respect and protect nature, as this is vital for our planet."

In the playground, Oliver tries everything:
swings, sandpit and climbing frames.
He happily plays with other children and patiently
waits for his turn at the slide if there is a queue.

Mummy warns Oliver that it is time to go home
in five minutes.
Mummy counts down to let Oliver
know how many minutes are left: 4-3-2-1-0.
At home, Mummy lets Oliver know that this is
his free play time, while Mummy prepares dinner.

Oliver plays with his trains, cars and roleplays
with his dolls. Sometimes he draws,
colors his books and writes letters.
Occasionally, he plays on his musical instruments.

Before dinner time, when Daddy is home,
Mummy, Oliver and Daddy go to the garden and
play some football, run in circles, or they race.
The family spends some quality time together.

During dinner time, Mummy, Daddy and Oliver
eat together and talk about their day.

After dinner, it is bath time.
Oliver plays with his toys in the bathtub,
such as dinosaurs, boats, water guns,
or blows bubbles with a cup and straw.

Oliver washes himself with soap to be
fresh and clean, and brushes his teeth to avoid
bad and painful teeth.

After bath time, Oliver and Daddy sit together on the
sofa, and watch cartoons. During this peaceful time,
Oliver becomes very relaxed and gets ready
for bedtime. Mummy warns Oliver he has five minutes
before he has to go to sleep. She starts counting down
to let him know how many minutes are left: 4-3-2-1-0.
Oliver says goodnight to Daddy, and gives him kisses.

Oliver chooses a book and Mummy reads some stories
for him. Oliver watches the pictures and comments on
the topic. "Goodnight, Oliver, I love you so much,
Mummy and Daddy are so happy that you are here
with us," says Mummy and holds Oliver's hand until he
falls asleep.

The end

Visual Cards

Feel free to cut out the following cards
to use as visual aids for your child...

Getting Up

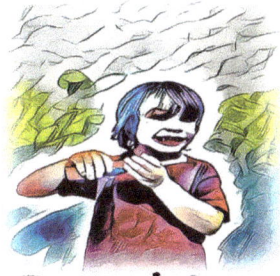

Brushing teeth

Screen time

Getting dressed

Breakfast

Nursery

Lunch

Bath time

Free play

Bedtime Story

Dinner

Off to sleep

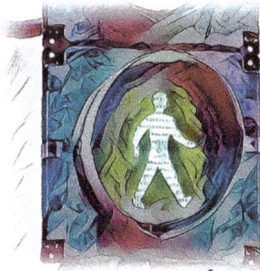

Road
Safety

Buggy

Playground

Scooter

Park

Bycicle/
Tricycle

Car

Shopping

Bus

Nappy/
Toilet

Train

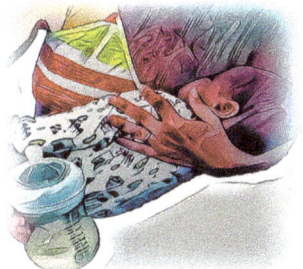

Milk

www.ingramcontent.com/pod-product-compliance
Lightning Source LLC
Chambersburg PA
CBHW040312050426
42452CB00018B/2812